Josh Brolin Biography

The Rise of a Hollywood Icon

Steven E. Barrios

Copyright © 2024 by Steven E. Barrios

All rights reserved. No part of this book may be reproduced, distributed, or transmitted in any form or by any means, including photocopying, recording, or other electronic or mechanical methods, without the prior written permission of the publisher, except in the case of brief quotations embodied in critical reviews and certain other noncommercial uses permitted by copyright law.

Table of contents

Introduction
Chapter 1: who is Josh Brolin
    The Man Behind the Icon
Chapter 2: Early Life and Roots
    Growing Up in California
    Family Ties: The Legacy of James Brolin
    The Call of Acting
Chapter 3: Breaking into Hollywood
    Early Roles and Struggles
    The Goonies: A Cult Classic Debut
Chapter 4: Career Renaissance
    Finding His Niche in Film and Television
    No Country for Old Men: A Career-Defining Role
    Becoming a Mainstay in Gritty Dramas
Chapter 5: The Marvel Era
    From Cable to Thanos: Dominating the Superhero Genre
    The Art of Playing Villains
Chapter 6: Personal Life and Challenges
    Overcoming Addiction and Personal Struggles
    Relationships, Marriage, and

Fatherhood

Chapter 7: Diverse Roles and Experimentation

   Exploring Comedy, Drama, and Everything In Between

   Collaborations with Hollywood's Best Directors

Chapter 8: Life Beyond Acting

   A Passion for Art and Creativity

   Advocacy and Philanthropy

Chapter 9: Legacy and Influence

   How Josh Brolin Redefined Longevity in Hollywood

   Inspiring the Next Generation

Conclusion

Introduction

In the entertainment world, Josh Brolin is a name that connotes adaptability and longevity. He has established himself as one of Hollywood's most renowned actors throughout the course of his decades-long career. Brolin has continuously shown his capacity to enthrall viewers, from his breakthrough performance in the cult classic The Goonies to his highly regarded roles in Milk and No Country for Old Men, as well as his famous portrayal of Thanos in the Marvel Cinematic Universe.

However, Brolin's tale is not limited to successful films and accolades. It is the story of a man who has persevered through personal and professional adversities, navigating the highs and lows of celebrity with fortitude and resolve. He has demonstrated his creative abilities beyond acting by pursuing his interests as a director and producer behind the camera.

This biography explores Josh Brolin's life and the significant events that have influenced his path. We'll learn the backstories of his most iconic roles and the events that shaped him as a person, from his childhood in a Hollywood household to his development as a diverse artist. Come honor the legacy of a genuine Hollywood legend whose creations never cease to amuse and inspire.

Josh Brolin's journey has been as rich, varied, and captivating as few Hollywood actors. From his early days as a young, undeveloped youngster in the popular 1985 adventure The Goonies to his iconic portrayal of the terrifying Thanos in the Marvel Cinematic Universe, Brolin has consistently demonstrated that his potential is limitless. He has gained critical recognition and a loyal following because of his ability to bring severely flawed, nuanced, and frequently fantastical characters to life.

However, there is a tale of tenacity, fortitude, and personal development hidden beneath the gloss and glamour of Hollywood. Brolin, who was born into a family of entertainers, could have easily coasted on his family name, but instead, he forged his road, which was filled with both successes and failures. He has experienced periods of professional stagnation, personal hardships, and self-discovery, all of which have influenced the actor and person we see today.

Brolin's path encompasses not only his on-screen accomplishments but also his personal development as a man. He is a devoted husband and father, a thoughtful thinker, and an artist who is always looking for new challenges, whether they involve working behind the camera, taking on parts that question conventional wisdom, or performing on stage. His filmography demonstrates his range and dedication to his profession, from the melancholic cowboy in No Country for Old Men to the revolutionary portrayal of Dan White in Milk.

An in-depth look at the man behind the classic roles is provided by this biography. It chronicles his ascent to stardom, the challenges he faced, and the legacy he is leaving behind in the entertainment sector. We'll look at his influences, his acting style, and the personal beliefs that have helped him navigate decades in the rapidly evolving Hollywood industry.

Josh Brolin's life is a tale of drive, perseverance, and artistic fervor; it is proof of the strength of accepting difficulties and remaining loyal to oneself. Discover the amazing journey of one of the most enduring stars of our time by delving into the pages that lie ahead.

Chapter 1: who is Josh Brolin

Josh Brolin is a well-known American actor and producer who has had an impressive career in Hollywood that spans many decades. Brolin was born in Santa Monica, California, on February 12, 1968, and was raised in an entertainment-related household. His stepmother, Barbra Streisand, is a legendary singer and actress, and his father, James Brolin, is a well-known actor. Josh carved out a career for himself in the field despite these connections, becoming known for his tenacity, adaptability, and commitment to his work.

Brolin's acting career started in 1985 when he played Brand Walsh, the older brother in the cult movie The Goonies.

His career in the film industry began with this role. Brolin's career had its ups and downs in the late 1980s and early 1990s, despite his early success. With notable roles in highly regarded movies like W. (2008), Milk (2008), and No Country for Old Men (2007), he did, however, have a notable comeback in the 2000s.

Brolin's portrayal as Thanos, the powerful and nuanced nemesis in the Avengers trilogy of the Marvel Cinematic Universe, has made him a household figure in recent years. His reputation as a Hollywood heavyweight was cemented when he was praised widely for his ability to humanize a fantastical villain.

Josh Brolin's versatility as an artist is demonstrated by his forays into producing and directing in addition to his cinematic work. His personal life, which has included well-recorded setbacks and victories, is equally well-known. Brolin, a husband and father, uses reflection and fortitude to strike a balance between his personal and professional lives.

Josh Brolin is one of the most admired and enduring performers of his time because of his story of tenacity, growth, and indisputable talent.

The Man Behind the Icon

Josh Brolin is a man who has embraced life's obstacles and victories with unyielding resolve; he is more than just a Hollywood celebrity. Even though his name is frequently linked to well-known figures and successful motion pictures, Josh Brolin's journey—one characterized by tenacity, creativity, and an unwavering quest for authenticity—is what defines him.

A man formed by his childhood and personal problems lies behind the strong performances and imposing on-screen demeanor. Brolin was born into a family with strong connections to the entertainment business, and his father's notoriety could have easily eclipsed him. Rather, he decided to pave his road, overcoming times of doubt and self-discovery in the process.

Brolin's life serves as an example of tenacity. He had both success and obscurity in the early years of his work, going through the highs of critical praise and the lows of few possibilities. He never quit, though. He came out stronger, honing his skills and establishing himself in a field that was always evolving. His steadfast perseverance turned him from a budding young actor in The Goonies to one of the most prestigious names in cinema, thanks to his parts in Milk, No Country for Old Men, and the iconic Thanos in the Marvel Cinematic Universe.

Josh Brolin is a thoughtful and complex individual off-screen. He has been candid about the significance of family in his life, his struggles with addiction, and his path to self-awareness. Even though he continues to take on challenging roles and new artistic challenges, he finds balance in the love and support of his family as a loving husband and father.

This period of his life and career serves as a reminder that icons are created via perseverance, diligence, and the guts to confront life's challenges head-on. Josh Brolin's tale is not only one of celebrity; it is also one of a man who has accepted the highs and lows to become a genuine artist and a very grounded person. The man behind the icon is this one.

Chapter 2: Early Life and Roots

Josh James Brolin was born into a family immersed in Hollywood customs on February 12, 1968, in Santa Monica, California. His mother, Jane Cameron Agee, was an independent spirit and a wildlife activist, while his father, James Brolin, was a well-known actor who had roles in movies and television. Josh grew up surrounded by the glamour of show business, but he also encountered its complications.

Brolin grew up on a ranch in Templeton, California, away from the limelight of Hollywood. His early years were a mix of natural charm and artistic family influence. He had a strong work ethic and a love of nature as a result of the simplicity of ranch life, traits that would help to define his grounded outlook as an adult. Brolin's early years were not characterized by privilege, despite his father's notoriety; his parents separated when he was a small child, and his mother's tragic death in a car accident when he was in his twenties had a profound effect on him.

Brolin didn't first find acting appealing as a teenager. Rather, he was captivated by the excitement of surfing and skating, and he spent a large portion of his childhood surrounded by California surf culture. He didn't realize how much he loved performing until he took part in a high school drama class. Brolin started to consider acting as a possible career route after being encouraged by a teacher who saw his innate skill.

Josh had a distinct perspective on life and his work because of his upbringing, which contrasted personal struggles with Hollywood's heritage. These early encounters would later influence the nuance and complexity he incorporated into his characters, enabling him to emotionally engage audiences.

His modest beginnings combined with a wealth of artistic inspiration paved the way for a career characterized by fortitude, self-reflection, and a passion for telling important tales. Josh Brolin's early years prepared him for his future as an actor and person, transforming him from a small-town ranch child to a worldwide celebrity.

Growing Up in California

Josh Brolin's early years in California were a combination of early exposure to the entertainment industry, personal development, and the state's natural beauty. Brolin's upbringing was influenced by both the grounding effect of country life and the glamour of show business. He was born in Santa Monica, a beachfront city renowned for its relaxed culture and proximity to Hollywood.

A large portion of Brolin's early years were spent on a ranch in Templeton, a tiny community in the Central Coast region of California. Josh's existence on the ranch was very different from the glamour of Hollywood, even though his father, James Brolin, was a well-known actor with parts in movies and television. Nature, exercise, and the strong work ethic that accompanied ranch life were the main focuses of this way of life. He developed a strong bond with the land and a love of simplicity during these formative years in the country, which would continue to be essential components of his adult perspective.

Brolin's early years were filled with inventiveness and curiosity, even though he wasn't instantly drawn to acting. Jane Cameron Agee, his mother, was both an artist and a wildlife activist. Her influence encouraged a love of the arts and a sense of independence. However, Josh first encountered the entertainment industry through his father's work. Though he didn't yet have any plans to follow in his father's footsteps, he was exposed to the rhythms of Hollywood and occasionally visited his film sets.

When Brolin was a teenager, his interests changed. He spent many hours outside developing his athleticism and became quite active in California's surf and skateboarding culture. He was deeply influenced by the carefree yet daring attitude of California in the 1980s. In particular, skateboarding gave him a way to express his creativity and energy, while the surfing culture fostered his sense of independence and community.

Brolin didn't discover his real acting vocation until high school. On a whim, he enrolled in a drama class, which led to his somewhat accidental discovery of theater. Brolin became enthralled with the art of acting after being inspired by a tutor who recognized his ability. His trajectory started to change in the direction of Hollywood at that point, and by the time he was in his late teens, he was prepared to leave the country life behind and venture into the busy streets of Los Angeles as a professional actor.

Brolin's upbringing in California offered him a special blend of urban potential and country innocence. His entertainment career was shaped by his experiences in both worlds, where he was surrounded by nature but also connected to Hollywood's creative spirit. From the California ranch to the Hollywood Hills, he underwent a journey of self-discovery, perseverance, and meaning-seeking that would ultimately influence the iconic roles he would play throughout his career.

Family Ties: The Legacy of James Brolin

Josh Brolin's father, James Brolin, was a veteran actor who had a distinguished career that spanned over half a century.

Without a doubt, Josh Brolin's introduction into the Hollywood industry was impacted by his father. In addition to leaving an indelible impression on the business, James Brolin's achievements in the film and television industries surely had a significant impact on his son's early life and the goals he went on to achieve.

At the beginning of his career, which began in the 1960s, James Brolin appeared in several notable parts in both film and television. As a result of his performance in the television series Marcus Welby, M.D. (1969-1976), for which he was awarded an Emmy Award, he gained widespread recognition. In addition, he had roles in several critically acclaimed films, including Westworld (1973) and The Amityville Horror (1979), as well as films that were released in the 1990s, such as Traffic (2000). His long-lasting success and presence in Hollywood made him a household figure but also placed him in the spotlight for much of Josh's early childhood.

Growing up, Josh was exposed to the realities of the entertainment industry—its expectations, its pressures, and the complicated balancing act between personal and professional life. Josh's connection with his father was one of equilibrium, even though he was immersed in the world of film sets and stardom. James' success in the industry could have easily cast a long shadow, but instead of resting on his father's popularity, Josh established his path.

In many ways, James Brolin's legacy served as both an inspiration and a challenge for his son. Josh was not given any preferential treatment in Hollywood, and his journey to fame was not an easy one. In reality, he often struggled with being seen as the son of a famous actor and had to prove his own worth in the field. However, James' career also offered Josh a clear example of the persistence, professionalism, and longevity needed to succeed in the entertainment world.

Despite their distinct paths, Josh and James shared a profound respect for each other. Their relationship is one of mutual appreciation, with Josh admitting his father's influence in his acting career. James, too, has expressed delight in Josh's accomplishments, especially in light of his son's ability to carve out his unique legacy.

In many respects, the Brolin family legacy continues to thrive in Hollywood. Josh's success might be considered an extension of his father's career, while it is equally a credit to his perseverance, talent, and personality. Both father and son have proved that the pursuit of an entertainment career is not simply about capitalizing on family connections but about the passion, drive, and authenticity one gives to their work.

Josh Brolin's journey in Hollywood is definitely characterized by the influence of his father, but it is his own story—his own obstacles, growth, and triumphs—that has truly defined his legacy. The relationship between them remains a cornerstone of his journey, a reminder of the profound family ties that shape and define his route to prominence.

The Call of Acting

Acting was a discovery that Josh Brolin made during his adolescence rather than an urgent goal. His first interests were elsewhere, even though he grew up in a family that was heavily involved in the entertainment sector. Far from the Hollywood world, Brolin's early interests were skating, surfing, and spending time in nature while growing up on a ranch in California. But Brolin first experienced the irresistible draw toward acting in a high school theater class.

Josh didn't initially think acting was his calling, even though his father had a well-known job in the entertainment sector. He was more interested in the freedom and exhilaration of sports, especially skateboarding, which was a major aspect of the young culture in California throughout the 1980s.

However, something happened in high school that made him, mainly on a whim, enroll in a theatrical class. He had a life-changing experience while performing in front of an audience in this setting.

Something clicked the instant he took the stage. The craft of presenting stories through acting enthralled Brolin. He found great resonance in the adrenaline of acting, the difficulty of assuming a different persona, the bond with an audience, and the emotional depth these characters evoked. What started as a fleeting interest quickly developed into a passion that would ultimately determine the course of his career.

As Brolin realized his new interest, he jumped into acting with a seriousness that matched his enthusiasm. He enrolled in acting classes and looked for performance chances since he took his trade seriously. He was still in his teens, but it soon became apparent that acting was more than simply a pastime. Brolin's commitment to his work helped him progressively rise above the shadow of his well-known father and forge his reputation in the business as he made his way through the rather bewildering world of Hollywood.

Josh's big break came in 1985 when he portrayed Brand Walsh, the oldest brother, in the well-known movie The Goonies. Even though the position did not initially constitute a significant turning point in his career, it did signal the start of his career. Brolin would later have to deal with the harsh realities of Hollywood, such as extended stretches of playing little parts and difficulties getting recognition as an actor. However, the want to act remained constant. He persisted in pursuing the art despite obstacles and self-doubt, gradually becoming known for his range and passion.

Brolin's dedication to acting throughout the years has earned him parts in highly regarded movies including True Grit (2010), Milk (2008), and No Country for Old Men (2007). His ability to play a variety of complicated roles, from the more human and tragic portrayal of Dan White in Milk to the brooding, ethically dubious Anton Chigurh in No Country for Old Men, brought him enormous praise and cemented his status as one of Hollywood's most esteemed actors.

Acting for Josh Brolin was not a passing fancy or a fortuitous turn of events. It was a profound, developing interest that started in high school classes and developed into a profession that would shape his life. From his early years of self-discovery to his ascent to fame in Hollywood, Brolin's path has been one of tenacity, commitment, and an unwavering quest for acting greatness.

Chapter 3: Breaking into Hollywood

Josh Brolin's journey into Hollywood was neither quick nor simple; rather, it was a slow one that was influenced by perseverance, education, and a dedication to improving his skills. Despite coming from a family with a long history in Hollywood—his father, James Brolin, was a well-known actor—Josh's entry into the business was characterized by his battle to establish his own identity and leave his well-known parent's shadow.

Brolin's first big break came in 1985 when he played Brand Walsh in the acclaimed adventure movie The Goonies, which was produced by Steven Spielberg. Josh's position as the protective elder brother was not the springboard for celebrity that some may have hoped for, despite The Goonies being a commercial triumph and a cultural icon. Instead, it served as a springboard for his recognition in the business, albeit Hollywood wasn't ready to give him major jobs right once.

Brolin found it challenging to make the move from child actor to adult roles after The Goonies, which is sometimes a challenging one in a field that tends to categorize young people. Throughout the late 1980s and early 1990s, he landed a variety of roles in movies and television, but they were sometimes unmemorable or didn't get the credit they merited. His performances on television programs such as Public Eye (1992) and The Young Riders (1989–1992) demonstrated his talent but did not propel him to the pinnacles of celebrity.

Brolin's career did not start to take off again until the late 1990s and early 2000s. He began to get increasingly significant and varied roles, which gave him the chance to show off the breadth and depth of his acting abilities. His role in the Coen brothers' No Country for Old Men in 2007 marked a sea change. Brolin's performance as Llewelyn Moss, a man entangled in a lethal game of cat and mouse with a psychotic hitman, was a masterwork of nuance and passion. Brolin's status was raised by the Academy Award-winning movie, and all of a sudden, he was regarded as a leading actor who could handle difficult, nuanced roles.

Brolin also played the younger George H.W. Bush in the films American Gangster (2007) and W. (2008) at this time. Hollywood started to take note of his variety as his career took off. Brolin received praise from critics and was nominated for an Academy Award for Best Supporting Actor for his portrayal of Dan White, the politician found guilty of the murders of Harvey Milk and George Moscone, in Milk (2008).

Even though Brolin's rise had been gradual, he had solidified his reputation as one of Hollywood's most dependable and adaptable actors by the time the 2010s arrived. His position as a worldwide celebrity was cemented when he played the antagonist Thanos in the Marvel Cinematic Universe, which started with Guardians of the Galaxy (2014) and ended with Avengers: Infinity War (2018) and Avengers: Endgame (2019). Despite being a computer-generated image, Brolin's motion-capture performance brought Thanos to life, demonstrating his capacity to play nuanced roles outside of the human world.

Josh Brolin had a hard time making his Hollywood debut. It required years of tenacity, negotiating the highs and lows of the entertainment business. After a noteworthy early appearance in The Goonies, he went on to be recognized in some of the most important 21st-century films. The success Brolin has today is the consequence of years of honing his art, selecting roles that pushed him, and creating a route that enabled him to become a well-known and esteemed actor in Hollywood. His journey is a monument to his commitment.

Early Roles and Struggles

Josh Brolin did not become a household name overnight. Despite having the advantage of being the son of renowned actor James Brolin, his early career was characterized by serious setbacks and a string of lackluster performances that failed to provide him with the acclaim he desired. Even if the business didn't recognize Brolin's promise right away, his early experiences helped to define his resolve to succeed. The road to Hollywood wasn't an easy one.

Josh Brolin's breakthrough performance as the protective older brother Brand Walsh in The Goonies (1985) catapulted him into the spotlight as a member of an ensemble cast in a hit movie. Brolin's subsequent years were marked by a series of forgettable appearances, many of which were on television, as The

Goonies did not instantly lead to a plethora of leading roles. Brolin starred in TV series such as Public Eye (1992), which received little recognition despite his excellent performances, and The Youthful Riders (1989–1992), a Western series that was a part of the youthful ensemble cast, for a large portion of the late 1980s and early 1990s.

Brolin was typecast in jobs at the time that didn't give him any opportunity to develop or show off his skills. Brolin found it especially difficult to make the shift from a kid actor to a more sophisticated, nuanced performer during this time. He had to confront the harsh fact that being a successful actor for a father could occasionally be more of a liability than a strength. In a society that frequently viewed him as "the son of James Brolin," rather than as a distinct actor with his special abilities and personality, he was always under pressure to prove himself.

During this time, there were both emotional and professional difficulties. Brolin struggled with self-doubt and the uncertainties that accompanied being a young actor in a field that did not tolerate people who were just starting. He worked for years to dispel the stigma associated with being a "young star" and demonstrate that he was more than just the Goonies' Brand. He began to wonder about his role in Hollywood as a result of this annoyance and the demands of the profession.

Nevertheless, in spite of the difficulties, these formative years had a significant role in molding Brolin into the actor he would become. They made him hone his skills, overcome moments of self-doubt, and discover the need for patience. Brolin has talked about how, throughout this period, he was devoted to developing his abilities since he knew that success would require years of sacrifice and hard effort. As he grew older, his resolve to move past his early positions enabled him to take on increasingly challenging and sophisticated tasks.

Brolin's career didn't start to change until the middle of the 2000s. His breakthrough came in 2007 with No Country for Old Men, in which he portrayed Llewelyn Moss, a man enmeshed in a perilous game of cat-and-mouse, following years of developing his talent in television and minor cinema roles. His tense and morally nuanced performance won him praise from critics and established him as a genuine actor who could handle challenging parts. However, Brolin was only able to secure jobs that demonstrated his breadth and aptitude after overcoming the initial difficulties of typecasting and limited opportunities.

Brolin's early professional setbacks had a significant impact on his growth as an actor. Even if the industry didn't see his talent right away, they taught him perseverance, patience, and the value of never stopping to improve his trade. These early years helped him become one of Hollywood's most renowned and adaptable actors, and they served as a vital basis for the more lucrative roles that would follow.

The Goonies: A Cult Classic Debut

Josh Brolin's big break came in 1985 when he was cast in The Goonies, a movie that would become a renowned cult classic in addition to influencing his early career. The Goonies, which Steven Spielberg and Richard Donner directed, encapsulated the spirit of teenage adventure in a way that would appeal to viewers for many years to come. Brolin portrayed Brand Walsh, Mikey's (Sean Astin) elder brother, who sets out with a gang of outcast children to uncover secret wealth and prevent the destruction of their houses.

Brolin's career in Hollywood began with his performance as Brand, even though The Goonies was an ensemble film with numerous young talents. He portrayed the protective, athletic, and occasionally disobedient older brother who eventually joins the youngsters on their crazy journey despite his early misgivings about the treasure search. Brolin's portrayal added humor and honesty to the movie, while Brand's character had the ideal mix of hardness and tenderness.

The Goonies proved a defining experience for Brolin, who was only 17 at the time of filming. In addition to introducing him to the camaraderie of working with a young ensemble cast, it gave him the chance to showcase his comedic timing and physicality, which would be useful in his future work. Notwithstanding its initial lackluster critical reception, the film's endearing and daring plot, along with its memorable ensemble of characters, helped it succeed at the box office and go on to become a cultural phenomenon.

The Goonies presented Brolin with both opportunities and difficulties. Although it gave him access to Hollywood, it also made him more closely associated with his character Brand in the eyes of the public, which later hindered his ability to move into more adult roles. According to Brolin, the movie was both a help and a hindrance because it labeled him as a "young, heroic" actor, which restricted his options in the years that followed.

The Goonies continue to be one of the pivotal events in Brolin's early career in spite of these difficulties. As the years went by and a new generation of fans discovered the movie through home video, TV broadcasts, and streaming services, its legacy only got stronger.

Since then, Brolin's portrayal of Brand has been acknowledged as one of the major factors in the movie's ongoing popularity.

The Goonies is one of the movies most closely linked to Josh Brolin, even though he would later play a wide range of characters. It opened his eyes to the world and, in many respects, the start of his lifelong connection to cinema, influencing his views on the medium and the business.

Brolin's part in The Goonies, which is now recognized as one of the most popular adventure movies of the 1980s, is a fundamental part of his early career. In addition to starting his Hollywood career, the movie cemented its legacy in popular culture. Brolin's portrayal of Brand continues to be a crucial component of The Goonies' allure as it continues to introduce new viewers to the wonders of juvenile adventure.

Chapter 4: Career Renaissance

Josh Brolin's career experienced a stunning comeback in the mid-2000s, following a string of early setbacks and being stereotyped as a young action star. This change was more than just a comeback to the limelight; it signaled the rise of a more experienced, adaptable performer who could handle challenging, multidimensional parts. Brolin's transformation from a forgotten teenage idol to a well-known character actor in Hollywood was characterized by several significant career decisions as well as a renewed emphasis on improving his craft.

When Brolin starred in the gritty, suspenseful Coen brothers' adaptation of Cormac McCarthy's novel, No Country for Old Men, in 2007, his career took a dramatic change. Brolin played Vietnam War veteran Llewelyn Moss, who becomes caught up in a deadly game of cat-and-mouse after discovering a cocaine deal gone awry. Brolin was able to depart from the more heroic or humorous parts he had previously been linked to by playing Moss with a quiet intensity and moral uncertainty. The movie won four Academy Awards, including Best Picture, and was a critical and financial success. Widespread praise for Brolin's performance solidified his standing as a serious, accomplished actor.

Following the popularity of No Country for Old Men, Brolin achieved yet another significant career turning point in 2008 when he played Dan White, the politician who killed Harvey Milk,

California's first out homosexual elected official. Brolin received his first Academy Award nomination for Best Supporting Actor for his depiction of White, which was marked by emotional complexity and a heartbreaking sense of inner conflict. His ability to portray complex, real-life characters was on full display in the performance, which also showed that he had developed as an actor beyond action movies and blockbusters.

Brolin's newfound fame was built upon in the ensuing years. He portrayed Tom Chaney, a man on the run for murder, in the critically acclaimed True Grit (2010), another film he co-starred on with the Coen brothers. Although Brolin's portrayal in True Grit was more sinister and evil than any of his previous roles, it also demonstrated his versatility in playing characters with a range of personalities and moral compass points.

Brolin also achieved success in popular movies throughout that decade, demonstrating his adaptability to both big-budget projects and smaller, highly-regarded movies. Beginning with Guardians of the Galaxy (2014) and ending with the multi-film saga that included Avengers: Infinity War (2018) and Avengers: Endgame (2019), his portrayal as the evil Thanos in the Marvel Cinematic Universe (MCU) garnered him international renown. Bololin used motion capture technology to bring the character to life as Thanos, a complex yet merciless figure with a grand plan to wipe out half of the universe's population to rescue it. The character's popularity and the MCU's worldwide influence made Brolin a household name and cemented his place among Hollywood's best actors.

Brolin's decisions during his professional comeback were characterized by a persistent desire to take on a range of parts that presented challenges to him in terms of complexity and scope. His roles in True Grit, Milk, No Country for Old Men, and the MCU demonstrated his ability to move fluidly between realistic drama and epic blockbusters. These parts showcased Brolin's extraordinary range as an actor, exhibiting a unique adaptability that distinguished him from his contemporaries.

Josh Brolin's career comeback is a tale of development, rebirth, and the strength of tenacity. Brolin's comeback to Hollywood as a versatile, well-regarded actor after years of fighting for recognition is evidence of his skill, diligence, and commitment. In addition to solidifying his status as one of Hollywood's best performers, Brolin has demonstrated that reinvention is achievable at any point in a career by starring in anything from gritty crime thrillers to huge superhero sagas.

Finding His Niche in Film and Television

The hallmark of Josh Brolin's career has been his flexibility, which has allowed him to adjust to the changing needs of Hollywood and carve out a distinct place for himself in both television and movies. Despite his early difficulties with typecasting and securing significant roles that suited his expanding repertoire, Brolin eventually found his niche in the business by concentrating on nuanced characters that struck a balance between strength and vulnerability and juggling well-known blockbusters with critically acclaimed dramas.

Brolin started embracing parts in the 2000s that gave him the chance to show off his acting abilities outside of the cliché of a young action hero. A major change in his career began with the success of No Country for Old Men (2007) and Milk (2008). His portrayals of ethically complex characters—often imperfect guys who operate in morally gray regions but are yet capable of depth and empathy—have earned him recognition. Brolin was a strong candidate for more complex, nuanced roles because of his performance as Llewelyn Moss in No Country for Old Men, a guy who finds a briefcase of money and stumbles into a dangerous world. In a similar vein, Brolin's portrayal of Dan White, the man who killed Harvey Milk, in Milk added to his expanding repertory and demonstrated his ability to capture the complexity and emotion of real-life characters.

Brolin's ability to handle bigger-than-life blockbuster franchises matched his transition to more intricate and emotional roles. His casting as the adversary Thanos in the Marvel Cinematic Universe (MCU) was a pivotal point in this change. Brolin was able to give the villain role a distinct gravitas by portraying the character with a profoundly philosophical attitude to his murderous objectives, even though the job required a great deal of motion-capture technology. By playing Thanos in multiple movies, including Guardians of the Galaxy (2014),

Avengers: Infinity War (2018), and Avengers: Endgame (2019), Brolin became well-known and cemented his position in both independent and big-budget studio franchises.

Brolin's career adaptability also made it possible for him to settle into television. He portrayed a complicated, ethically torn character in the 2015 season of the critically acclaimed television series The Dilemma, which explored the effects of choices made in interpersonal relationships. His ability to play characters in complex and high-pressure situations complemented television's changing landscape, as series like Breaking Bad and True Detective demonstrated to viewers that television could have just as much depth as movies.

Brolin's portrayal of George Hearst, a notorious Old West magnate, in the Western crime series Deadwood (2004–2007) further demonstrated his ability to manage complex, historical characters. Brolin was able to examine themes of power, greed, and morality through the show's realistic and gritty depiction of the American frontier, which was a perfect fit with the growing trend of television adopting more mature, character-driven programming.

Brolin has established himself in Hollywood as an actor who can move fluidly between the two worlds by finding a balance between big-budget franchises and more personal, tragic parts in independent and television films. His career demonstrates a capacity to strike a balance between financial success and artistic integrity; he frequently chooses parts that are both demanding and give him the chance to delve into the intricacies of human nature.

Through television and movies, Brolin's journey is one of self-discovery and growth. He has embraced a range of parts that challenge his skills and enable him to engage with a broad audience, rather than being restricted to a single genre or character type. His career is a reminder that in a field as big and cutthroat as Hollywood, it takes a combination of flexibility, tenacity, and a dedication to selecting jobs that resonate on a personal and professional level to find one's place. Brolin has established a varied and prosperous career in the entertainment industry by combining dramatic drama, fantastical villains, and iconic TV performances.

No Country for Old Men: A Career-Defining Role

Josh Brolin became one of Hollywood's most acclaimed and versatile performers with his performance in No Country for Old Men (2007), which was a turning point in his career. Based on Cormac McCarthy's book, Joel and Ethan Coen's bleak, violent crime thriller delves into issues of fate, morality, and the breakdown of conventional ideas of justice. Brolin's role as Llewelyn Moss, a regular guy who finds a bag full of drug money, leads to a lethal chase with a resolute sheriff named Ed Tom Bell (played by Tommy Lee Jones) and an unrelenting hitman named Anton Chigurh (played by Javier Bardem).

For several reasons, Brolin's portrayal of Moss is a performance that defines his career. First of all, Llewelyn Moss is not your average hero. A working-class man with a strong sense of self-preservation, he finds himself in a predicament that is becoming more and more perilous and morally dubious. Brolin portrayed Moss with a cool, collected intensity, never exaggerating the character's resolve or terror. His portrayal, which is subdued but captivating, captures the inner conflict of a man torn between the repercussions of his decisions and his wish for a better life.

To play the part, Brolin had to compete with more seasoned actors like Jones and Bardem, who both delivered outstanding performances. Brolin's portrayal of the hunted man was just as powerful as Bardem's terrifying portrayal of the sociopath Chigurh, which received worldwide praise and an

Academy Award for Best Supporting Actor. His subtle yet powerful portrayal of Moss served to ground the movie and made it possible for the violence and tension to develop in a more nuanced, relatable manner. Moss became one of the most memorable characters in the movie because of his ability to elicit quiet heroism through morally challenging times, stoic resilience, and moments of indecision.

The movie marked a sea change in Brolin's career as a whole, not just for him. With four Academy Awards, including Best Picture and Best Director, No Country for Old Men was a critical and financial triumph that solidified the Coen brothers' status as modern filmmaking greats. Brolin received considerable appreciation for his depiction of Moss, earning nominations for other top awards, despite not winning an Oscar for the part. Many people consider his performance in No Country for Old Men to be among his best, demonstrating his ability to portray nuanced, ethically torn characters with an amazing harmony of nuance and restraint.

No Country for Old Men also signaled the start of a new stage in Brolin's career, one in which he would be in high demand for roles that were more complex and character-driven. The movie's popularity helped him break away from his previous Hollywood roles, which frequently positioned him as the action hero or the tough guy. Brolin demonstrated that he was capable of handling roles considerably more complex and nuanced than those he had been assigned in his early career by immersing himself in a realm of existential wondering and merciless violence in No Country for Old Men.

Brolin's ability to play parts that required both physicality and emotional nuance was also underlined in the Coen brothers' film. Although he displayed moments of unadulterated survival instinct in his portrayal of Moss, he never lost sight of the character's inner turmoil. Brolin's reputation as a serious, talented actor was cemented by this balance, which distinguished him from other performers of his generation.

As Brolin's career grew in the years after No Country for Old Men, he took on a wider range of parts in television and movies, such as the highly regarded Milk (2008) and his eventual participation in the Marvel Cinematic Universe. But many people believe that Brolin came into his own as a top-tier actor who could compete in both indie and big-budget productions with the character of Llewelyn Moss.

In the end, Josh Brolin's performance in No Country for Old Men marks not only a career turning point but also a chance to escape previous typecasting and showcase his entire skill set. The movie is a tribute to his acting prowess and continues to be one of his most recognizable parts.

Becoming a Mainstay in Gritty Dramas

Josh Brolin was firmly established as a go-to actor for dark, emotional dramas after his career-defining role in No Country for Old Men. A string of prominent, frequently sinister parts followed the success of his depiction as Llewelyn Moss, a morally complicated guy trapped in a harsh, cruel environment. Brolin was a natural choice for the increasingly popular gritty drama genre, which emphasizes moral ambiguity and emotional conflicts, because of his ability to inhabit characters that are flawed, conflicted, and intensely real.

Milk (2008), which was directed by Gus Van Sant, was one of the most important turning points in Brolin's evolution into this new stage. Brolin portrayed Dan White, the former politician who killed Harvey Milk (Sean Penn), California's first out homosexual government official, in this biographical drama. White was portrayed by Brolin as a man struggling with inner turmoil, annoyance, and ingrained prejudice in a frighteningly nuanced way. He received a lot of praise from critics for his portrayal, which led to his first nomination for Best Supporting Actor at the Academy Awards. By examining his reasons and humanizing a character who is frequently perceived as a villain, this part demonstrated his ability to put himself in the shoes of a real-life person.

After Milk, Brolin kept establishing himself as a major force in realistic, character-driven dramas. Brolin portrayed the evil Tom Chaney in the Coen brothers' 2010 film True Grit, a fugitive whose brutal deeds set the scene for the tale of justice and retribution. Brolin once again showed his ability to give darker characters nuance, even though his role was smaller than his performance in No Country for Old Men. He was a powerful opponent in the movie because of his portrayal of Chaney, which demonstrated his ability to strike a balance between brawn and emotional depth.

Brolin played Detective Sergeant John O'Mara in the stylized crime drama Gangster Squad, which was set in 1940s Los Angeles, in 2011. The emergence of organized crime and a group of LAPD officers' attempts to apprehend infamous criminal Mickey Cohen were both covered in the movie. Brolin's performance of O'Mara, a gruff yet moral police officer, demonstrated his increasing ease in parts that required both a tough exterior and a sharp emotional edge. Brolin's performance was one of the film's main highlights, and it was noteworthy for its fusion of traditional noir elements and contemporary sensibilities.

Brolin's position in the gritty drama genre was further cemented when he discovered a lucrative outlet in television in addition to his career in feature films. He starred in Aaron Sorkin's historical legal drama miniseries The Trial of the Chicago 7 in 2015. Brolin was essential in this series' examination of the tumultuous political landscape of the 1960s, encapsulating the angst and militancy of the era. He was a perfect choice for novels involving social and political upheaval because of his ability to give characters who were confused and morally complex depth and realism.

There are several reasons why Brolin continues to be successful in tough dramas. First, he distinguishes himself in a genre that relies on moral ambiguity by playing characters who are difficult to identify as good or bad. He is a dependable choice for characters in high-stakes, frequently violent situations where the characters' internal struggles reflect the exterior ones they encounter because of his physicality and acute emotional sensitivity.

Furthermore, Brolin frequently chooses parts in harsh dramas with a purposeful emphasis on content rather than style. He has managed to avoid being categorized into roles that are only based on his popularity or physical attributes. Rather, he has opted to collaborate with forward-thinking filmmakers and screenplays that enable him to go deeper into more captivating tales of human nature, frequently revolving around themes of justice, survival, and retribution. He has been able to keep up a new and captivating presence in Hollywood by accepting challenging and morally dubious parts.

The evolution of Brolin's career following the triumph of No Country for Old Men is evident in his transition into a staple of grim dramas. He developed a varied body of work that has garnered him both critical acclaim and a devoted following by embracing complex, multifaceted characters in a range of genres, from crime thrillers to historical dramas. As one of Hollywood's most dependable and captivating performers today, Josh Brolin is renowned for his ability to give even the most dramatic and dark parts depth and gravity. His reputation as a mainstay in gritty dramas is solidly established, demonstrating his extraordinary versatility and commitment to the genre.

Chapter 5: The Marvel Era

Another significant turning point in Josh Brolin's career was his entry into the Marvel Cinematic Universe (MCU), which not only made him famous throughout the world but also cemented his status as a multifaceted actor who can handle both intricate, nuanced performances and big-budget blockbuster roles. The role of the powerful antagonist Thanos, who would go on to become one of the most recognizable characters in superhero movie history, marked Brolin's entry into the MCU in 2014.

Brolin's MCU debut was everything but typical. Instead of portraying a conventional human persona, he used state-of-the-art motion capture technology to bring the enormous antagonist Thanos to life. The character made a brief but significant debut in Guardians of the Galaxy (2014). At first, Thanos was presented as an aloof, all-powerful character whose mission to acquire the Infinity Stones would play a major role in the MCU's overall storyline. Despite having a little part in Guardians of the Galaxy, Brolin's performance set the stage for a character who would eventually determine the course of the whole Marvel world.

The ability of Brolin to give Thanos a depth and intellectual sophistication that is uncommon for villains in comic books was what made his interpretation of the character stand out. Thanos's motivations stemmed from a perverted sense of cosmic balance rather than from straightforward greed or the desire for dominance. He felt that he had to exterminate half of all life to prevent the universe from becoming overpopulated and destroyed. Brolin's portrayal of Thanos gave him a feeling of tragedy and inevitable fate, and this idealistic yet terrifying vision provided a moral rationale for his homicidal deeds. Thanos was motivated by the belief that he was the only one who could carry out the necessary actions, even if it meant giving up everything, and it wasn't just about being evil for the sake of evil.

The success of Avengers: Infinity War (2018) and Avengers: Endgame (2019), two of the highest-grossing movies ever made, was greatly influenced by Brolin's portrayal of Thanos. The main story point of Infinity War revolved around Brolin's Thanos, the main antagonist, and his pursuit of the six Infinity Stones.

Brolin's motion capture performance gave the character a terrifying presence on film, making him both physically intimidating and emotionally significant. Thanos felt less like a villain and more like a force of nature—unstoppable and fatalistic—because of his deep voice and measured delivery, which gave him a cool, collected manner that made him even more terrifying.

Brolin's Thanos emerged as the quintessential representation of sacrifice and devastation in Avengers: Endgame (2019). His persona posed a danger not just to the Avengers but also to the cosmos as a whole. Thanos is a tragic and dangerous character in Endgame because of his readiness to suffer personal tragedy to achieve his objectives. The character's eventual defeat in the movie was both emotionally poignant and fulfilling because of the emotional weight Brolin brought to the part. His portrayal of Thanos made him one of the most interesting and memorable characters in the MCU by giving the viewers a villain with emotional depth and internal anguish in addition to creating the tension required for the Infinity Saga's finale.

Brolin's performance as Thanos in the MCU catapulted him into the A-list of Hollywood actors and gave him a new degree of international notoriety. Unquestionably, the character had a cultural impact, and Brolin's portrayal of Thanos became one of the most acclaimed depictions of a comic book villain in contemporary film. The actor is now regarded as one of Hollywood's most adaptable characters, able to take on both the most difficult serious roles and the greatest blockbusters, thanks to his work in the MCU.

In addition to Thanos, Brolin's tenure in the Marvel universe has shown his openness to adopting novel roles and embracing new technologies. Brolin's role as Cable, a time-traveling antihero with a complicated past, in Deadpool 2 (2018) solidified his place as a pivotal character in the comic book film genre. Although Cable was a more conventional, human character than Thanos, he nevertheless needed the same kind of nuance and dedication to character development for which Brolin had gained a reputation. His portrayal of Cable demonstrated his versatility and ability to move fluidly between villains and antiheroes while still making a significant impact in movies with a range of moods and aesthetics.

Brolin has contributed to more than one legendary figure in the MCU. He demonstrated his ability to handle the challenges of both funny and serious material by playing two very different characters in the same genre in Deadpool 2 and Avengers: Infinity War. Even as he pursued roles in independent dramas and films, his work in the MCU helped him to maintain his position as a major player in Hollywood.

Josh Brolin's career throughout the Marvel Era is not just about his appearances in popular movies; it also shows how he has developed as an actor and taken on parts that push his emotional and physical range. In particular, Thanos emerged as a pivotal role that demonstrated Brolin's range as an actor and his ability to give the superhero genre a sense of gravity. Brolin's performance in the MCU demonstrated that he could not only compete in a world where spectacle and computer-generated imagery rule, but also elevate these tales with his nuanced portrayal of one of the most iconic and complicated villains in movie history.

From Cable to Thanos: Dominating the Superhero Genre

Josh Brolin's entry into the superhero genre was nothing short of revolutionary, since he was able to create two memorable performances in radically different characters within the same genre: Thanos in the Marvel Cinematic Universe (MCU) and Cable in

Deadpool 2 (2018). His portrayal of these opposing personas demonstrated his range as an actor and solidified his standing as a major player in the superhero movie industry.

In Deadpool 2, Brolin played Cable, a seasoned time-traveling soldier who is determined to change the past and preserve his family's future. A well-liked character in Marvel Comics, Cable is renowned for his tragic past, commanding strength, and no-nonsense demeanor. Brolin successfully portrayed these qualities by striking a mix of toughness and nuanced sensitivity. His portrayal contrasted sharply with Ryan Reynolds' humorous and irreverent Deadpool, establishing a dynamic that deepened the humor and action in the movie. While moments of reflection showed a man profoundly impacted by grief and duty, Cable's steely manner and relentless purpose made him an engaging counterpoint to Deadpool.

Brolin's ability to keep Cable grounded in reality despite the film's outrageous humor and hectic action scenes is what made the role so unforgettable. Cable's status as a futuristic warrior was given more credibility by his dramatic physical metamorphosis for the part, which included a muscular build and a grizzled, battle-worn appearance. Because of Brolin's deadpan delivery and his chemistry with Reynolds, Cable was able to strike the ideal balance between being a grudging ally and a dangerous foe. Brolin's performance served as an emotional underpinning, ensuring that Cable was more than just a parody of a tough guy, even though Deadpool 2 leaned primarily toward comedy.

At the same time, Brolin was assuming the iconic character of the Mad Titan, Thanos, in the MCU. Thanos was a villain with a godlike presence and a philosophical commitment that distinguished him from other antagonists, whereas Cable was based on human tragedy. The main plot of Avengers: Infinity War (2018) and Avengers: Endgame (2019) revolved around Thanos's attempt to acquire the six Infinity Stones and "restore balance" to the universe. Brolin used motion capture technology to make Thanos come to life, giving a performance that combined emotional nuance with physical menace.

Brolin's ability to provide humanity to a figure who, on paper, could have easily been a one-dimensional evil is what made his Thanos so famous. Thanos was presented as a fervent idealist who felt his genocidal scheme was required for the sake of the greater good, despite his horrific deeds. Thanos was given a sense of gravity by Brolin's composed, cool portrayal, which made him a villain who was simultaneously horrifying and somehow likable. Audiences were able to see the internal turmoil that drove his character through his quiet intensity and vulnerable moments.

Brolin's multiple personas as Thanos and Cable demonstrated his extraordinary versatility in the superhero genre. He portrayed a gritty, grounded antihero who was motivated by personal loss, on the one hand. Conversely, he portrayed a villain with cosmic-scale ambitions who was larger than life. Although physicality and passion were necessary for both personas, their performance requirements differed. Brolin handled these difficulties with ease, producing two unique and memorable performances.

The popularity of these parts also demonstrated Brolin's flexibility in responding to the changing needs of the superhero genre. Characters that were emotionally nuanced, morally complicated, and essential to their particular stories were welcomed by Brolin as the genre grew beyond straightforward good-versus-evil tales. Strong acting is still crucial in a genre that is dominated by spectacle and extraordinary effects, as seen by his performances, which enhanced the movies in which he starred.

In addition to their respective achievements, Cable and Thanos represented the duality of Brolin's career at this time. He helped create the legacy of the MCU as Thanos, the face of one of the most massive film ventures ever. He also demonstrated his versatility by adding depth to a more self-aware, irreverent series in his role as Cable.

Josh Brolin's dominance in the superhero genre is evidence of his acting prowess and capacity to bring complexity to even the most fanciful parts. In addition to contributing to the legacy of these well-known characters, his performances of Cable and Thanos showed his dedication to giving each performance nuance and realism. Brolin demonstrated that even in a universe full of fantastical heroes and villains, the human element is what really connects by dominating the superhero genre with such powerful performances.

The Art of Playing Villains

Josh Brolin is a genius at portraying villains; he gives parts that could easily be reduced to caricatures a sense of nuance and complexity. In a genre that is sometimes characterized by sharp distinctions between good and evil, his capacity to humanize villains and expose the complex causes underlying their actions has distinguished him. Brolin treats villains as complex people influenced by circumstance, conviction, or moral ambiguity rather than as the silent threat of Thanos in the Marvel Cinematic Universe or the icy, cunning figures in his dramatic work.

The ability of Brolin to evoke sympathy for people who carry out heinous deeds is among the most captivating features of his evil depictions. Despite not being a villain in and of himself, his character's decisions in No Country for Old Men (2007) set him up for conflict with Anton Chigurh, one of the most dreadful antagonists in movies. Brolin's later work in evil parts was made possible by his comprehension of the moral complexities and stakes involved. His conviction that every antagonist views oneself as the protagonist of their tale was strengthened by this early encounter, and he applies this idea to all of his nasty roles.

The Relatable Titan, Thanos

Brolin's portrayal of Thanos is a masterwork of villainy in the MCU. Brolin gave the Mad Titan a calm conviction and an almost tragic sense of purpose instead of portraying him as a stereotypical megalomaniac. Thanos thought that eradicating half of the universe to avoid shortage and overpopulation was a necessary evil. Even though Thanos' tactics were reprehensible, Brolin's nuanced acting forced viewers to consider the unsettling idea that he might have a point.

Brolin gave Thanos a distinct humanity with motion-capture technology, making sure the character's existence was not obscured by the visual effects. In scenes like his sorrowful sacrifice of Gamora, his subtle gestures and facial expressions revealed an unexpected tenderness. Thanos became one of the most interesting adversaries in movie history thanks to his combination of pathos and threat, which took him above the level of a standard comic book villain.

Milk's Dan White: A Terrifying Real-Life Evil

Brolin played Dan White, the man who killed Harvey Milk, California's first openly homosexual public official, in the 2008 film Milk. Brolin refrained from depicting White as a one-dimensional monster, even though his deeds were unquestionably evil. Rather, he explored the fears, annoyances, and social pressures that pushed White to carry out his horrible deeds. Brolin received a nomination for Best Supporting Actor at the Academy Awards as a result of his spooky and incredibly disturbing performance.

By examining Dan White's humanity, Brolin brought attention to the perilous junction of individual shortcomings and social discrimination, transforming the character into a metaphor for more significant cultural problems. Brolin's technique of portraying antagonists is distinguished by its capacity to relate specific villainy to more general concepts.

Adrian Pryce's ruthless complexity and Oldboy

Brolin portrayed Adrian Pryce in the 2013 Oldboy adaptation, a villain whose heinousness stemmed from intense personal suffering and an unquenchable thirst for vengeance. Despite the film's negative reviews, Brolin's performance was notable for its depth of emotion and intensity. Brolin created a villain driven by unbridled, unadulterated emotion as Pryce, a character whose deeds were both horrific and intensely personal.

From the Viewpoint of a Villain

Brolin's reluctance to pass judgment on his characters is what makes him unique. He takes an empathetic approach to each part, trying to comprehend the motivations behind their choices, no matter how sinister. Because of this way of thinking, he can see the humanity in even the most heinous characters, which deepens the impact of his performances. Brolin makes sure his antagonists are never overly simple, whether it's Adrian Pryce's ruthless retaliation, Dan White's fears, or Thanos' philosophical conviction.

According to Brolin, villains are the most fascinating characters to portray because they compel performers to delve into the most sinister aspects of human nature. Brolin provides both the bravery and the accuracy needed for this exploration. His skill at portraying villains resides in his ability to make viewers comprehend—if not empathize with—the behaviors of the characters, turning even the most heinous characters become incredibly captivating examinations of human frailties.

A Master Villain's Legacy

Josh Brolin's status as one of Hollywood's most talented actors has been solidified by his ability to give his opponents life. He has shown that antagonists are frequently at the center of a story's conflict and emotional weight, serving as more than just barriers for heroes to overcome. Brolin has reinvented what it means to play a villain with his performances, demonstrating that the most memorable villains are those that force viewers to consider the world from their point of view, even if only briefly.

Chapter 6: Personal Life and Challenges

Josh Brolin's magnetism on television and strong performances belie a life filled with struggles and personal victories. Brolin's off-screen path is a monument to tenacity and development, as she navigates the highs and lows of celebrity and overcomes personal obstacles.

Life in the Family

Josh was raised in a creative and passionate environment, which influenced his appreciation of the arts and the intricacies of family relationships. He was born to actor James Brolin and animal activist Jane Cameron Agee. Family has always been a foundation in his life, guiding his decisions and keeping him rooted in the fast-paced world of Hollywood.

Trevor and Eden, the two children from Brolin's first marriage to actress Alice Adair, marked the beginning of his fatherhood. Brolin has talked about the value of keeping tight ties with his kids despite the challenges of his rapidly growing career. His marriage to model Kathryn Boyd, with whom he has two daughters, has stabilized and brightened his personal life in recent years. In contrast to the intense roles he plays on screen, Brolin frequently posts glimpses of his family life on social media, showing a softer, more intimate side.

Addiction Struggles
Brolin struggled with substance problems in his early years, just like many other people in Hollywood. He has

been candid about his struggles with drugs and alcohol, which started when he was young and lasted into adulthood. Brolin has discussed how these difficulties impacted his personal and professional life in interviews, acknowledging that beating addiction was one of his biggest obstacles.

He took action to address his problems and pursue a healthy lifestyle after realizing that a change was necessary. An encouraging feature of his story is his readiness to face these obstacles head-on and embrace sober. Fans have responded well to Brolin's candor regarding his past hardships, which emphasizes his bravery and sincerity.

Public scrutiny and legal issues

Brolin has also been the subject of public scrutiny at times, including legal run-ins. Arrests for bar fights and a public scuffle in his younger years are noteworthy instances. These incidents, which were frequently emphasized by the media, put Brolin's fortitude and capacity to overcome hardship to the test. He focused on his craft and personal development as he attempted to restore his reputation over time.

In retrospect, Brolin has characterized these difficulties as chances for reflection and change. They turned into pivotal events that influenced his outlook on life and how he handled relationships in both his personal and professional life.

Striking a Balance

As Brolin's career took off, he looked for methods to reconcile his desire for a fulfilling personal life with the demands of Hollywood. He attributes his ability to remain grounded to his family and his passion for outdoor pursuits like farming and hiking. In addition to performing, Brolin has cultivated a strong love of literature and the arts, which give him a creative outlet.

This new equilibrium is largely the result of his marriage to Kathryn Boyd. Boyd's encouragement and support are frequently praised by Brolin, who calls their friendship a source of strength. With their girls at the center of their happiness, they have created a life together that is centered on family, creativity, and personal development.

Resilience's Legacy

The story of Josh Brolin's personal life is one of perseverance, change, and atonement. He has approached life's obstacles with an openness that motivates others, from his battles with addiction and legal issues to the delights of parenthood and family. Brolin is now praised not only for his acting but also for his sincerity and capacity to transform setbacks into learning experiences. His life story serves as a lesson that one may find strength, fulfillment, and purpose even when faced with hardship.

Overcoming Addiction and Personal Struggles

Josh Brolin faced many obstacles in his path to becoming one of Hollywood's most renowned performers. Beyond his professional gloss and glamour, there is a very personal tale of resiliency and self-discovery. Brolin's battles with addiction and inner turmoil had the potential to ruin his life and career, but his ability to face these problems head-on and learn from them is a remarkable testament to tenacity.

The Initial Challenges

Long before he was well-known, Brolin was battling addiction in his early years. He was exposed to the negative aspects of living in a fast-paced setting while growing up in California. Brolin has openly discussed in interviews how his adolescence was characterized by drug and alcohol experimentation, which resulted in tendencies that would last into maturity.

Brolin's use of drugs during these early years caused him to personally witness the effects of addiction. He has acknowledged committing dangerous crimes, such as stealing and careless partying, which he has explained as a coping mechanism for his fears and the demands of figuring out who he is. These early encounters laid the groundwork for what would eventually develop into a major personal conflict.

The Effects of Addiction on His Life
Addiction became a persistent problem for Brolin as his career took off. His alcohol dependence was made worse by the demands of Hollywood as well as the emotional toll of his personal life, which included his divorce from actress Alice Adair. Even though Brolin kept up a steady career in television and movies, he has admitted that his battles with addiction frequently influenced his relationships and impaired his judgment.

His arrest in 2008 after a brawl in a Louisiana bar while filming W. was one particularly noteworthy low point. Along with earlier well-publicized run-ins with the law, this episode demonstrated how his problems were starting to affect the public. These incidents acted as wake-up calls, forcing Brolin to face the deeper problems that motivated his actions.

Shifting the Waves

Although Brolin's road to recovery was not a straight line, it was characterized by a strong desire to change. He accepted the path of recovery and sought assistance after realizing the toll addiction was having on his personal and professional life. This process included mental and emotional healing in addition to physical rehabilitation.

Brolin's decision to prioritize accountability and introspection marked a sea change. He threw himself into his career, using acting as a cathartic outlet and directing his energies into his skills. He was able to go deeply into the emotional ground in roles like those in Milk and No Country for Old Men, which mirrored his introspective journey.

Brolin also took comfort in relationships and family. A new chapter in his life, one characterized by stability and support, began in 2016 when he married Kathryn Boyd. They created a life together that was based on mutual understanding, growth, and love. Their two girls have grown to be Brolin's inspiration and source of happiness, which has strengthened his resolve to lead a sober and healthy life.

Knowledge Acquired

Speaking frankly in interviews about the value of self-awareness and getting assistance, Brolin has been transparent about the lessons he learned during his fight with addiction. He attributes his rehabilitation to a mix of personal willpower, professional assistance, and the steadfast support of family members.

Brolin highlights the value of confronting one's issues rather than avoiding them in his reflections on his path. According to him, maintaining sober is a daily exercise that calls for integrity, modesty, and a readiness to change. Even in the face of seemingly insurmountable odds, recovery is possible, as his experience reminds us.

Motivating Others

Josh Brolin has inspired innumerable fans and peers with his ability to overcome addiction and personal challenges. His candor regarding his prior struggles dispels the stigma associated with addiction and acts as a ray of hope for people going through comparable struggles. In addition to being a well-known actor, Brolin is now seen as a representation of tenacity and forgiveness.

Brolin has demonstrated by his journey that obstacles in life may be transforming rather than defining. His narrative emphasizes the value of tenacity, self-compassion, and the conviction that it's never too late to make a difference. Brolin consistently shows that real strength comes from facing hardship head-on and coming out stronger on the other side, whether on or off-screen.

Relationships, Marriage, and Fatherhood

Josh Brolin's experiences in relationships, marriage, and fatherhood have shaped his personal life, which has been a path of introspection, growth, and intense love. Even while his work has frequently put him in the spotlight, what makes him unique is his commitment to his family and interpersonal relationships.

Early Connections and Knowledge Acquired

In 1988, Brolin wed actress Alice Adair for the first time, and the two of them had two children: Trevor and Eden. Brolin has remained close to his children despite the couple's 1994 divorce. During this period, he has talked positively about being a father, calling it a life-changing experience that changed his outlook. Brolin remains dedicated to being there for his children despite the difficulties of juggling a growing career with parental duties.

Brolin's personal relationships had ups and downs following his first marriage, including a high-profile engagement to actress Minnie Driver that ended in 2001. Despite their challenges, these encounters gave Brolin the chance to consider his personal development and what he desired in a mate.

Diane Lane's Marriage: A Complicated Chapter
Actress Diane Lane and Brolin were married in 2004, and their union soon won praise from the press and fans.

Given their mutual respect for one another's art and their love of acting, the couple seemed to be a natural match. But there were difficulties in their marriage.

After Brolin was arrested for domestic violence in 2004, the relationship came under public scrutiny; however, both Brolin and Lane later played down the incident, calling it a misunderstanding. Despite their attempts to manage the demands of Hollywood life and marriage, the pair finally got divorced in 2013. Since then, Brolin has characterized this phase of his life as a time of personal development, during which he learned important lessons about self-improvement, communication, and accountability.

A Fresh Start with Kathryn Boyd

Brolin's personal life entered a new phase of stability and contentment in 2016 when he wed model and former aide Kathryn Boyd. Mutual support and a love of adventure have been hallmarks of the couple's relationship. Brolin has frequently commended Boyd for her upbeat attitude and impact on his life, seeing her as a stabilizing influence that enabled him to adopt a more balanced and healthful way of living.

Westlyn Reign, born in 2018, and Chapel Grace, born in 2020, are their two daughters together. Brolin gives viewers an insight into his role as a loving husband and father by often posting touching moments with his family on social media.

Fatherhood: An Essential Function

Being a father has been one of the most significant parts of Josh Brolin's life. His world revolves around his children, both from his previous marriage and his current one. Fatherhood has influenced Brolin's outlook on life and love, which he has characterized as a humble and fulfilling experience.

Brolin has adopted a hands-on approach with his younger girls, rediscovering the pleasures of parenthood. He has voiced his appreciation for the chance to become a father at various points in his life, pointing out that becoming older has made it possible for him to be a more intentional and present parent.

Managing Work and Family
Brolin prioritizes family time despite his hectic work, frequently choosing the peace of home life over the bustle of

Hollywood. Brolin constantly highlights the value of family in his life, whether it's through sharing touching posts about his kids or being candid about the lessons he's learned from his relationships.

He has also acknowledged that his wife and kids have motivated him to work on projects that align with his principles and leave a lasting legacy for his family. His subsequent years are now characterized by this harmony between his personal contentment and professional aspirations.

A Tradition of Love and Development
Josh Brolin's marriages, relationships, and fatherhood serve as examples of his path toward resilience and personal development. Every stage of his life—from the thrills of a new romance to

the difficulties of divorce and introspection—has influenced the man he is now. His steadfast devotion to his family and his capacity to grow from his experiences have endured throughout it all.

Brolin's tale is one of self-discovery and metamorphosis in addition to sexual relationships. It is evidence of the strength of love, responsibility, and the will to create a meaningful and connected existence. One of the most fascinating facets of Brolin's life is his legacy as a loving father and partner, even while he succeeds both on and off screen.

Chapter 7: Diverse Roles and Experimentation

Josh Brolin's career is evidence of his unafraid acting style. He has taken on a variety of roles over the years, demonstrating his adaptability and readiness to try out different genres and media. Brolin has consistently pushed himself to explore new storytelling elements, frequently pushing outside of his comfort zone to give memorable performances in everything from cult classics to blockbuster blockbusters and small independent films.

From a supporting role to the main character

Brolin's breakthrough performance in The Goonies (1985) was one of many supporting parts he was given early in his career. But soon, he showed a variety that went well beyond the clichéd "tough guy" persona. He demonstrated that he could compete as a leading man by examining complicated, nuanced characters in movies like Milk (2008) and No Country for Old Men (2007).

These performances demonstrated Brolin's capacity to blend in with his parts while simultaneously showcasing his dramatic depth. He captivated spectators with his honesty and dedication, whether he was portraying a seasoned detective, a conflicted cowboy, or a historical character.

Getting the Hang of Gritty Dramas
Brolin, who frequently plays parts that delve into the darker aspects of human nature, has come to be associated with grim dramas. His ability to play ethically complex characters is seen in his roles in

movies like Oldboy (2013) and Sicario (2015). Brolin conveys a fierce intensity in these parts, striking a balance between emotional sensitivity and physical hardness.

His ability to humanize even the most imperfect characters is what makes him unique. As he negotiates the ambiguous morals of the war on drugs, for example, his performance of a crafty government agent in Sicario is both terrifying and yet empathetic.

Trying Out Comedies and Lighthearted Parts

Although Brolin's tragic roles are his most well-known, he has also demonstrated an unexpected talent for comedy. A notable divergence from his typical work was his portrayal of Bigfoot Bjornsen in Inherent Vice (2014), which demonstrated his comic timing and willingness to embrace quirky characters.

Brolin portrayed Cable in Deadpool 2 (2018), a time-traveling soldier whose somber manner stood in sharp contrast to the irreverent humor of the movie. The performance gained depth and refinement from his ability to strike a balance between the story's comic components and his character's serious tone.

Entering the Superhero World Bololin's entry into the superhero genre demonstrated his versatility even more. He revolutionized what a comic book villain could be with his portrayal of Thanos in the Marvel Cinematic Universe. Brolin used motion-capture technology to give the character a depth and gravity that went beyond what is usually expected of the genre.

At the same time, his performance as Cable in Deadpool 2 showed that he could infuse superhero movies with a distinct energy by fusing physicality with a dry sense of humor that went well with Ryan Reynolds' anarchic Deadpool.

Accepting Independent Films

Brolin has remained closely associated with independent film throughout his career, accepting jobs that allow for more in-depth artistic experimentation. Movies such as W. (2008), when he played President George W. Bush, demonstrate his readiness to take on difficult and contentious roles. Brolin's reputation as an actor who isn't afraid to try new things is further cemented by the fact that these movies frequently provide him the chance to take artistic chances.

Physical Change and Dedication

Brolin's physical changes for different roles demonstrate his dedication to his job. He trained hard to play the powerful and muscular Cable in Deadpool 2, and he immersed himself in the harsh surroundings of the movie's setting to portray the character's realism in No Country for Old Men.

This commitment also extends to his emotional readiness. Brolin frequently explores his characters' psychology in great detail, which adds nuance to his performances. His commitment and artistic integrity are demonstrated by his ability to enter a role completely, whether it be that of a frightening villain or a sorrowful antihero.

A Tradition of Courage and Adaptability

Josh Brolin's reputation as one of Hollywood's most versatile performers has been cemented by his readiness to take on a variety of parts and try out various genres. His career is a testament to his unwavering quest for development, as every position presents a fresh challenge and a chance to broaden his creative horizons.

Whether tackling dramatic dramas, humorous comedies, or action-packed blockbusters, Brolin never fails to enthrall and astonish viewers with his performances. His legacy is one of adaptability, bravery, and a lifelong dedication to the performing arts. It's impossible to predict where his artistic path will take him as he keeps taking on new tasks.

Exploring Comedy, Drama, and Everything In Between

Josh Brolin's career is a masterwork of adaptability, showcasing his ability to move between genres with ease and give fascinating performances in all of his roles. Brolin has consistently pushed boundaries, demonstrating his diverse talent and courageous approach to acting, from his early days in poignant dramas to unexpected turns in quirky comedy.

Dramatic Origins: Developing Emotional Complexity

A pillar of Brolin's work has always been his dramatic narrative background. His breakthrough performance in The Goonies (1985) and other early roles suggested that he was naturally charismatic, but his performances in

Milk (2008) and No Country for Old Men (2007) solidified his reputation as a dramatic force.

Brolin's portrayal of Dan White, the torn politician whose actions had devastating effects on the LGBTQ+ community, was disturbing in Milk. He was nominated for an Academy Award for the part, which demonstrated his ability to play morally complex characters with delicacy and depth. Brolin's dedication to examining his characters' weaknesses and bringing a genuine and likable humanity to the screen frequently accounts for his success in dramas.

Entering the Comedy Industry: A Perfect Fit

Although Brolin's career has primarily focused on drama, his forays into humor show a lighter, more lighthearted side that viewers have grown to enjoy. He played Bigfoot Bjornsen in the 2014 film Inherent Vice, a straight-laced, eccentric detective with a ridiculous sense of humor. Brolin's deadpan delivery and willingness to embrace the character's quirks produced some of the most memorable scenes in the movie.

His portrayal of Cable in Deadpool 2 (2018) also struck a balance between the somberness of a seasoned combatant and a subtle, dry sense of humor. His relationship with Ryan Reynolds gave the action-packed superhero movie an unexpectedly humorous touch, demonstrating that Brolin could compete in a comedy-focused franchise.

His off-screen interviews and social media presence, where he frequently exhibits a keen wit and self-deprecating humor, further solidify Brolin's comedic instincts and win over fans.

Combining Genres to Get the Best of Both

Brolin's ability to transcend genres is what makes him unique; he frequently blends comedy and drama to produce characters that are completely developed. For instance, in W. (2008), he skillfully portrayed President George W. Bush's eccentric nature by fusing humor with moving scenes to produce a complex portrait that was both sympathetic and critical.

His performance in the Coen Brothers parody Hail, Caesar! (2016) further showcased his ability to strike a mix between tragic undertones and humorous timing. Brolin, who played a struggling Hollywood fixer, handled the ridiculousness of the movie's narrative with ease and gave a blend of seriousness and humor to the part.

Trying My Hand at Action and Superhero Movies

Brolin stands out in action and superhero movies due to his strong presence. His performance as Thanos in the Marvel Cinematic Universe, which blends the solemnity of a Shakespearean antagonist with nuanced emotional overtones, is a career-defining accomplishment. Thanos is one of the most interesting and memorable characters in the genre because Brolin gives the character vulnerability even though he is the adversary.

His performance as Cable in Deadpool 2, on the other hand, made extensive use of physicality and stoicism while preserving humor. His ability to adjust to the demands of large-scale productions without sacrificing the emotional essence of his characters is demonstrated by these performances.

The Craft of Trial and Error

One of Brolin's best qualities is his willingness to try new things. He has made sure that no two roles are the same by embracing independent films, blockbusters, and everything in between. Brolin constantly pushes the limits of his art, whether he is portraying a tough government agent in Sicario (2015), a distraught parent in Everest (2015), or a bizarre Western cowboy in the television series Outer Range (2022).

His artistic method reflects this spirit of adventure as well. Brolin is renowned for losing himself in his roles, frequently changing both physically and emotionally to give his performances more realism.

A Career in Range and Contrast

Josh Brolin's ability to succeed in every genre has characterized his career. He has shown a daring dedication to narrative in all its forms, from powerful dramas and suspenseful action movies to quirky comedies and avant-garde indies. His portrayals frequently combine depth, humor, and emotion to create characters that are memorable long after the credits have rolled.

Brolin's status as one of Hollywood's most dynamic actors will live on thanks to his ability to embrace a variety of genres and his ongoing exploration of new characters. Every new project offers viewers a chance to see a master at work, repeatedly demonstrating that his versatility is unbounded.

Collaborations with Hollywood's Best Directors

Working with some of the most gifted and innovative filmmakers in the business has influenced Josh Brolin's remarkable career. In addition to improving his performances, these collaborations have strengthened his standing as an actor who gives each project depth and dedication. Under the tutelage of Hollywood's finest, Brolin has continuously flourished, from the Coen Brothers' brilliant narrative to Denis Villeneuve's audacious ideas.

The Coen Brothers: Producing Hardy Works of Art
One of the most important collaborations in Brolin's career has been

with Joel and Ethan Coen. No Country for Old Men (2007), their debut joint effort, was a turning point for Brolin. Brolin gives a quiet but impactful performance as Llewelyn Moss, a man who discovers a fortune and becomes the target of a ruthless killer. This performance served as the foundation for the film's gripping plot. Brolin's portrayal of the tough everyday man and the Coen Brothers' careful directing made the movie a critical and financial triumph, winning four Academy Awards, including Best Picture.

With True Grit (2010) and Hail, Caesar! (2016), the collaboration persisted. Brolin portrayed the desperate bandit Tom Chaney in True Grit, giving the part a frightening yet sympathetic appeal. He demonstrated his comedic abilities in Hail, Caesar! as Eddie Mannix, a

Hollywood fixer who manages mayhem on a studio lot. These movies demonstrate Brolin's flexibility in adjusting to the Coen Brothers' distinct style of combining humor, drama, and character-driven narrative.

Denis Villeneuve: Examining Complicated People

Brolin has also collaborated extensively with Denis Villeneuve, a filmmaker renowned for his strikingly beautiful and emotionally stirring movies. Brolin portrayed Matt Graver, a shady government agent negotiating the hazy morals of the drug war, in the 2015 film Sicario. Brolin gave a complex performance under Villeneuve's guidance that struck a mix between brutality, charm, and moral ambiguity.

Their partnership continued in Dune (2021) when Brolin played the devoted and ferociously protective warrior Gurney Halleck. Brolin was able to explore a more heroic and stoic role in Villeneuve's epic adaptation of Frank Herbert's book, demonstrating his versatility in a narrative that was expansive and visually stunning.

Oliver Stone: Dealing with Differing Opinions

Brolin has the chance to take on the role of one of America's most divisive personalities by working with Oliver Stone. He played President George W. Bush in W. (2008), a position that called for both emotional nuance and physical change. Brolin's dedication to recreating the subtleties of Bush's personality and Stone's unwavering devotion to political commentary produced a portrayal that was both critical and sympathetic.

This partnership was a turning point in Brolin's career because it showed how sensitively and intricately he could handle difficult, real-life characters.

Paul Thomas Anderson: Exploring Surreal Comedy

Brolin's collaboration with Paul Thomas Anderson on Inherent Vice (2014) demonstrated his ability as a comedian in a delightfully quirky story. As the well-dressed but ridiculous investigator Bigfoot Bjornsen, Brolin welcomed the film's frantic energy and oddball humor. Brolin was able to experiment with a persona who was at once humorous, frightening, and somehow charming thanks to Anderson's distinct filmmaking approach.

Ridley Scott: Succeeding in Dramatic High stakes

In American Gangster (2007), Brolin costarred with Ridley Scott as Detective Trupo, a dishonest police officer caught up in the criminal underworld. Brolin's ability to play morally dubious roles and Scott's painstaking attention to detail made him an intriguing addition to the film's ensemble cast, which also comprised Russell Crowe and Denzel Washington.

The Russo Brothers and James Gunn: Creating the Modern Supervillain

Brolin collaborated with filmmakers James Gunn and the Russo Brothers to create Thanos in the Marvel Cinematic Universe. Brolin's portrayal of Thanos, one of the most recognizable antagonists in movie history, revolutionized the superhero genre in Avengers: Infinity War (2018) and Avengers: Endgame (2019). Brolin gave Thanos a sense of gravity by drawing inspiration from the Russo Brothers' skill at striking a balance between intense character moments and expansive action sequences. This resulted in a complex enemy whose motivations were just as fascinating as his destructive deeds.

Partnerships with Up-and-Coming Directors

Additionally, by giving his celebrity and expertise to films that could otherwise go unnoticed, Brolin has supported up-and-coming filmmakers. His collaborations with filmmakers like Megan Ellison and JC Chandor (producer of All Is Lost) show his dedication to promoting daring, unorthodox narratives.

A Tradition of Artistic Exploration and Trust

Josh Brolin's work with Hollywood's top directors is indicative of a career based on artistic inquiry, adaptability, and trust. Brolin has continuously produced performances that enhance the content and enthrall viewers, whether collaborating with seasoned auteurs or up-and-coming artists. His versatility as a director and performer highlights his reputation as one of the most versatile members of his generation.

Brolin's reputation as a collaborator and storyteller is still a major factor in his long-term success in Hollywood, as he continues to work with innovative filmmakers.

Chapter 8: Life Beyond Acting

Josh Brolin is most recognized for his long and diverse career in movies, but his life outside of acting is just as vibrant and reflects his interests, passions, and development as a person. Beyond the big screen, Brolin's career is distinguished by his devotion to his family, charitable giving, and a personal resolve to overcome hardship. His interests outside of acting enhance his legacy and provide a more in-depth look at the man behind the roles.

Fatherhood and Family Life

Brolin's current self has been greatly influenced by his family. Brolin, who is the father of three children from other partnerships, frequently talks positively about his upbringing and the principles they taught him. He takes his duty as a father extremely seriously, and his off-screen life is frequently centered around his kids.

Brolin wed actress Kathryn Boyd in 2016, and the two of them had two kids. He has found personal stability and happiness in his relationship with Boyd, and the two of them regularly post peeks of their lives together on social media. Brolin has embraced parenting with a refreshing candor, candidly talking about the pleasures and difficulties of juggling his well-known work with his family life. One of his most important characteristics is his dedication to being there for his kids and creating a loving environment.

Overcoming Individual Challenges

Throughout his life, Brolin has dealt with a variety of personal issues, chief among them being substance abuse. Brolin struggled with addiction as a child, and his journey to recovery has played a significant role in his development as a person. In addition to being important for his profession, overcoming these obstacles allowed him to gain a better understanding of who he was.

He has been candid about his difficulties and has used his narrative to encourage those who deal with the same problems. Because of Brolin's openness about his past, discussions regarding addiction and mental health have become less stigmatized in Hollywood, where these subjects are frequently ignored. His sober path is evidence of his tenacity and has influenced his outlook on both life and his career.

Giving Back and Philanthropy

Beyond his work and family, Brolin is committed to philanthropy and using his position to help issues that are important to him. He is especially involved in promoting animal rights, environmental sustainability, and programs that aid impoverished people. Beyond his career accomplishments, his desire to make a positive impact on the world is frequently the foundation of his humanitarian activities.

Brolin has donated his time and resources to causes that share his views and is active in several organizations. He has partnered with several environmental organizations because of his enthusiasm for protecting endangered species and wildlife. Because of his own experiences, he has also been active in helping groups that encourage addiction recovery.

Pursuit of Interests and Hobbies

Brolin maintains his sense of groundedness through a range of interests and pastimes outside of his acting job and philanthropic activity. His passion for the great outdoors is evident in his love of hiking, fishing, and horseback riding. A significant part of his life has been his relationship with nature, and he frequently posts pictures of his outdoor experiences on social media.

Brolin also has a strong interest in the arts, especially painting and photography. He frequently expresses himself through visual storytelling, and he has shared some of his own creations on a variety of sites. Through this creative outlet, he may express his artistic side in a way that enhances his acting profession by providing a balance between the personal freedom of creation and the focused focus of performance.

Business ventures

Brolin has dabbled in entrepreneurship in addition to his artistic and charitable endeavors. Over the years, he has made investments in a number of commercial endeavors, such as those pertaining to fitness, health and wellness, and even real estate. His business ventures are a reflection of a larger desire to create a financially and personally satisfying existence outside of Hollywood.

A Man of Introspection and Development

Beyond performing, Brolin's life is characterized by self-reflection, personal development, and a desire to live a genuine existence. He is a man who is always changing, as evidenced by his journey through personal struggles, his devotion to his family, and his commitment to giving back to the community.

As Brolin's career develops, it becomes evident that his personal life is just as intricate and multifaceted as the characters he plays on screen. He keeps evolving, changing, and motivating others who follow his path with every year that goes by. His efforts to live a well-rounded, purposeful life that goes well beyond the spotlight have also influenced his legacy, in addition to his parts in movies.

A Passion for Art and Creativity

Josh Brolin's artistic development goes well beyond his on-screen personas. Brolin is a very imaginative person who uses art in all of its forms as a vehicle for self-expression and self-discovery. His dedication to creation, which ranges from storytelling and poetry to painting and photography, shows his complex personality and his wish to establish a deeper connection with the world.

Examining Visual Arts: Photography and Painting

A recurring theme in Brolin's life has been his passion for visual art. He has frequently discussed how painting gives him a therapeutic outlet that lets him express his feelings and ideas in a manner that acting cannot. A distinct aspect of his creativity—one that is intensely introspective and intimate—is shown in his paintings, which span from abstract compositions to emotionally charged ones.

Likewise, one of Brolin's greatest passions has been photography. He frequently posts snippets of his work on social media and is well-known for taking eye-catching pictures. His images typically highlight the beauty of nature, ordinary life, and unguarded human moments, demonstrating his attention to detail and understanding of the nuances of his surroundings.

Using Writing to Tell Stories
Writing is another way that Brolin expresses his creativity. His use of language, whether in poems, short tales, or introspective essays, reflects the

nuance and complexity of his performance. His writing frequently explores themes of self-discovery, growth, love, and grief, giving readers an insight into his inner life.

In order to share his introspective thoughts with a larger audience, Brolin has indicated interest in publishing a compilation of his works at some point. In addition to demonstrating his artistic aptitude, his ability to tell stories is a continuation of his love of storytelling, which has been central to his acting career.

The Confluence of Acting and Art

For Brolin, acting and art are closely related. He has frequently compared his role-playing preparation to the process of making a work of art, where he meticulously layers reasons, details, and emotions to give a character life. He has been able to produce performances that are genuine and profound because of his creative approach to his work.

Brolin's other artistic endeavors are likewise influenced by his experiences as an actor. His writing and visual art frequently draw inspiration from the feelings and tales he depicts on screen, generating a creative feedback loop that enhances every facet of his output.

Using Art as a Reflective and Healing Tool

Brolin's artistic pursuits serve as a tool for introspection and rehabilitation, going beyond simple pastimes. He has used painting as a means of processing his feelings and gaining perspective during times of personal struggle or transformation. Brolin finds comfort and meaning in creating, whether it's with a brushstroke on canvas or a shutter click on a camera.

His outlook on life has also been impacted by this passion, which has inspired him to accept flaws and see the beauty in being vulnerable. Brolin's development as a person and an artist is ongoing via his work.

Motivating Others to Be More Creative
Brolin is a devoted artist who frequently inspires people to pursue their artistic endeavors. He highlights the value of artistic expression as a tool for self-discovery and connection, whether through open interviews, social media posts, or discussions with fans.

Brolin's artistic career serves as a reminder that there are no limits to creativity. In addition to improving his own life, he has encouraged numerous people to follow their artistic aspirations by embracing his artistic inclinations.

An Unwavering Dedication to Art

Josh Brolin views art as a way of life rather than just a hobby. From his well-received performances to his artistic endeavors, his love of creativity permeates all he does. Brolin is still a living example of the transformational potential of art and its capacity to unite us with the world and ourselves as he continues to experiment with new forms of expression.

Advocacy and Philanthropy

Beyond his career as an actor, Josh Brolin is known for his strong advocacy and philanthropic work, emphasizing subjects close to his heart. Brolin has turned into a voice for change, using his notoriety to affect the world, whether it is by supporting addiction recovery, advocating for animal rights, or using his platform to increase awareness of environmental issues. His advocacy is a sincere desire to further the common good and encourage others to follow suit, and it goes beyond his public persona.

Promoting Environmental Sustainability
Brolin is a fervent environmentalist who has promoted environmental conservation initiatives by using his prominence. He has been vocal about the need for more accountability in preserving the environment, especially when it comes to problems like deforestation, climate change, and the depletion of natural resources.

Brolin has been an outspoken advocate for protecting the environment because of his passion for the natural world, which stems from his enjoyment of outdoor pursuits like hiking and fishing. He backs several environmental groups, such as those devoted to protecting species and their habitat. By promoting sustainable behaviors in their personal lives and on a broader, policy-driven level, Brolin inspires his followers and peers to be more conscious of their environmental impact.

Protection and Rights of Animals
Additionally, Brolin has grown to be a fervent supporter of animal rights. He regularly speaks out against animal abuse on social media, especially when it comes to factory farming, poaching of wildlife, and the treatment of domesticated animals. His campaigning

aims to bring about real change rather than only increasing awareness.

Brolin has raised money and supported projects that aim to save animals from dangerous situations and give them better lives by collaborating with several animal rescue groups. His support of these projects demonstrates his profound compassion for animals and his dedication to enhancing their well-being.

Assistance with Addiction Recovery
Brolin is a fervent supporter of anyone battling substance misuse and addiction, having personally dealt with addiction. In addition to normalizing discussions about addiction, his candor about his battles with the disease has given many people facing comparable challenges hope.

To inspire others to get treatment, Brolin has shared his story with groups that specialize in addiction recovery. Those battling substance misuse have found encouragement in his path to sobriety, and he frequently discusses the value of mental health, self-awareness, and personal development in overcoming addiction. Brolin has been instrumental in lessening the stigma associated with addiction by openly sharing his challenges and recovery.

Promoting Awareness of Mental Health
Brolin is an ardent advocate for mental health awareness as well as addiction treatment. He has been frank about the difficulties and demands of being in the spotlight as well as the significance of having an open and judgment-free

conversation regarding mental health concerns.

Supporting programs that foster self-care, advance mental wellness, and offer services to those in need of psychiatric assistance are all part of Brolin's involvement in this area. His attempts to de-stigmatize mental health conditions are a reflection of his conviction that well-being and personal development are equally as vital as physical health.

Assistance to Underprivileged Areas
Brolin's charitable endeavors include aiding impoverished people, especially those who require access to economic, medical, and educational opportunities. He has collaborated with NGOs that offer aid and resources to underserved

populations, such as refugees and underprivileged children.

In addition to giving money, Brolin uses his time and voice to promote equality and social justice as part of his humanitarian endeavors. He has collaborated with groups that work to give people who are homeless or living in poverty food, shelter, and protection.

Events and Contributions to Charities
In addition to his advocacy work, Brolin participates in a lot of fundraising events and charity causes. He has raised money for numerous charities by taking part in charity performances, galas, and benefit auctions. These gatherings give him the chance to network with like-minded people in the entertainment sector and beyond who share his passion for improving the world.

Brolin's commitment to charity is reflected in his financial donations, where he has contributed to several causes that share his beliefs. His kindness has significantly improved the lives of several needy people and underprivileged communities.

A Tradition of Giving Back

Josh Brolin's reputation as someone who uses his platform for the greater good has been solidified by his dedication to advocacy and philanthropy. Brolin's influence goes well beyond the entertainment sector, whether it is through his support of addiction rehabilitation, his involvement in environmental conservation, or his continuous initiatives to raise awareness of mental health issues.

Brolin is an example of how people, particularly those with prominent public profiles, may use their influence to promote positive change in the world as he continues to advocate for vital causes. The strength of giving back is demonstrated by his charitable legacy, which is based on empathy, sincerity, and a desire to change the world.

Chapter 9: Legacy and Influence

Josh Brolin's personal and professional lives have had a lasting impact on the entertainment business and society at large. Brolin's impact extends well beyond Hollywood, from his starring roles in classic movies to his support of environmental and humanitarian concerns. Brolin's history as an actor, philanthropist, and creative person is characterized by fortitude, adaptability, and a dedication to changing the world for the better.

A Multifaceted and Influential Career in Acting

Brolin's reputation as an actor is largely based on his versatility since each character has struck a chord with viewers for a variety of reasons. Brolin has consistently pushed the limits of his art, from his early breakthrough in The Goonies to his career-defining roles in the Marvel Cinematic Universe and No Country for Old Men. He has established himself as one of Hollywood's most admired actors thanks to his representations of nuanced characters, whether they be villains, antiheroes, or damaged people.

His roles in the superhero genre, especially as the powerful Cable in Deadpool 2 and the all-powerful Thanos in the Avengers movies, have made him a mainstay of contemporary film and have attracted new audiences. At the same time, his performances in character-driven stories, Westerns, and gritty dramas have demonstrated his versatility. Brolin's career serves as an example of how an actor can stay regarded and relevant in a variety of genres and eras, and his dedication to being true to each part guarantees that his influence will last for many years to come.

Dispelling Myths and Putting Expectations to the Test

The fact that Brolin has defied expectations and broken preconceptions is one of the most important parts of his legacy. Early in his career, he was frequently referred to as Hollywood's "bad boy," a reputation he reversed by carefully selecting parts that gave him the chance to delve into the subtleties of characters that weren't merely stereotypical villains. By stepping outside of conventional clichés and presenting audiences with more complicated and compelling characters, Brolin's willingness to play challenging, ethically dubious roles has helped to expand our perception of what it means to be a leading man in Hollywood.

Furthermore, Brolin's professional path casts doubt on the notion of Hollywood's "star-making machine" by demonstrating that success isn't always correlated with instant celebrity or widespread acceptance. His tenacity in assuming a variety of roles—sometimes after early setbacks—illustrates the value of tenacity, creativity, and adaptability.

Effect on the Way Villains Are Represented in Hollywood

How adversaries are portrayed in modern movies has been greatly impacted by Brolin's depiction of villains, particularly Thanos in the Avengers series. His portrayal of Thanos, who is profoundly philosophical and, in his opinion, justifiable for his devastating deeds, contributed to the villain role's increased complexity, which is uncommon in popular superhero movies. Brolin's subtle portrayal gave the villain role more complexity than was previously seen in many blockbuster movies, presenting Thanos as a force of nature with goals derived from his warped sense of justice rather than just an evil figure.

The way that movie studios today handle their adversaries is one way that Brolin's effect may be observed. Brolin was part of a movement that helped define the idea that villains are no longer merely there to function as roadblocks for heroes; they are now fully developed characters with their moral compass.

A History of Social Change and Advocacy

Brolin's career is greatly influenced by his activism and charitable endeavors off-screen. As someone who genuinely wants to use his public position for good, he has used his platform to promote causes that are important to his heart, such as animal rights, addiction rehabilitation, mental health awareness, and environmental protection. Through his continuous involvement and support, Brolin has demonstrated his genuine dedication to these causes, going beyond the occasional charity event.

His candor regarding his battles with addiction has had a particularly significant influence. Brolin has been an ambassador for mental health and addiction recovery by openly facing and overcoming these obstacles, empowering others to get assistance without feeling ashamed. Many people have found hope in his tale, which has also helped to lessen the stigma associated with substance misuse and mental health problems in Hollywood and society in general.

An Integrated Impact on the Arts

Brolin has an impact on the arts in addition to acting and charity. His love of literature, photography, and the visual arts is a reflection of his drive to express himself in a variety of ways. Brolin has demonstrated via his side endeavors and artistic channels that pursuing art is a lifetime endeavor that continues long after the camera stops rolling. His contributions to different fields have encouraged others to pursue their artistic pursuits and serve as a reminder that creativity is not limited to a single medium or line of work.

The Impact on Upcoming Actor Generations

Additionally, Josh Brolin's career leaves a lasting impression on individuals in the entertainment industry and aspiring performers. He has shown how crucial adaptability, tenacity, and genuineness are to establishing a successful and fulfilling profession. Young performers looking to negotiate the demands and difficulties of Hollywood might learn from his determination to take chances and never stop pushing himself creatively. Brolin's example demonstrates that genuine professional success stems from an unrelenting dedication to one's craft despite challenges or uncertain times.

A Durable Legacy

Josh Brolin left behind a legacy that is deep and enduring. He has made a lasting impression on the film industry as an actor, renowned for his remarkable range and capacity to evoke strong emotions in viewers long after the credits have rolled. His dedication to changing the world is evident in his campaigning and personal development, demonstrating that his impact goes well beyond his on-screen personas. Brolin's legacy serves as a reminder that genuine artistry transcends all disciplines and that leading a meaningful life involves creativity, purpose, and a commitment to leaving the world in a better state than when we found it.

How Josh Brolin Redefined Longevity in Hollywood

A masterclass in redefining longevity in Hollywood may be found in Josh Brolin's career. In a field that is known for its transient nature—where stars frequently shine brightly but then fade—Brolin's capacity to remain current and consistently develop has made him one of the most enduring personalities in contemporary film. His professional path demonstrates how an actor may redefine what it means to make a lasting impression in Hollywood while simultaneously maintaining prosperity.

Accepting Flexibility in Role Choosing
Brolin's longevity can be attributed in large part to his extraordinary range as an actor. Brolin has consistently pursued a variety of characters, ranging from

nuanced supporting roles to villains, morally dubious antiheroes, and heroic figures, rather than adhering to a particular role type. His career has remained interesting and dynamic due to his desire to play a wide range of roles in genres like humor, action, drama, thriller, and even animation.

Brolin established himself in television early in his career with programs like Private Eye and The Young Riders. He took care to avoid being restricted to any one kind of job, though, which helped him avoid the professional stalemate that many actors encountered following their initial breakthrough. His roles in highly regarded movies like American Gangster, True Grit, and No Country for Old Men contributed to his reputation as an actor who could handle the most complex and difficult parts.

More recently, Brolin was introduced to a whole new generation of moviegoers through his roles as the antihero Cable in Deadpool 2 and the legendary villain Thanos in the Marvel Cinematic Universe. He has been at the top of Hollywood's talent pool for decades because of his ability to switch between serious dramas and popular franchises with ease.

Developing Your Reinvention Skills
Brolin's capacity for self-reinvention has also distinguished his career. He experienced times of insecurity and career lulls, like many young actors. Instead of letting these setbacks define him, Brolin took use of them to try new things, hone his skills, and recover stronger.

Following his early successes in the 1980s and 1990s in movies like The Goonies and The Fugitive, Brolin was cast in several parts that didn't showcase his abilities. He did, however, use this time to concentrate on character development and establish himself as a professional actor. His pivotal parts in movies like Milk (2008), where he was nominated for an Academy Award for his depiction of Dan White, and No Country for Old Men (2007), where he received critical acclaim for his portrayal of Llewelyn Moss, marked the culmination of this time of maturation.

These parts demonstrated that Brolin was a versatile actor who could grow and change with his craft and the characters he played, rather than being a one-dimensional performer. One of the main reasons he has stayed a mainstay of Hollywood for so long is his capacity to reinvent himself following early setbacks.

Strategic Career Choices and Partnerships

Brolin's long career can also be ascribed to his methodical and selective project selection process. He has collaborated with some of the most well-known directors throughout his career, including Quentin Tarantino (Grindhouse), Ridley Scott (American Gangster), and the Coen Brothers (No Country for Old Men), guaranteeing that his work is constantly in line with elite creative teams.

Working with these filmmakers helped him establish himself as an actor with a wide variety of appeals in addition to improving his performances. Brolin's versatility and ability to provide substance to any character have made him a sought-after collaborator on a variety of films, including high-octane action movies, morally complicated dramas, and suspenseful thrillers.

Furthermore, Brolin has benefited greatly from his participation in the Marvel Cinematic Universe, which has drawn older viewers who are familiar with his earlier work while also introducing him to new ones. Despite the significant use of computer graphics, Brolin's portrayal of Thanos was a performance triumph because he gave humanity to a character who could have easily been reduced to a one-dimensional evil. Brolin's sustained relevance has been guaranteed by his astute franchise participation, demonstrating that being relevant in

Hollywood requires not avoiding big movies but rather actively engaging with them.

Developing a Character Actor's Reputation

Another important factor in Brolin's long career has been his transition from a conventional leading man to a character actor. While many actors become well-known due to their charisma or physical attractiveness, Brolin's career was dependent on his ability to play complex, deeply flawed characters. Instead of focusing solely on "good guys" or "bad guys," his roles frequently highlight multifaceted personalities.

For example, his portrayal of George W. Bush in W. (2008) was a risky decision because it called for him to humanize a divisive public figure without compromising nuance. In No Country for Old Men, Brolin portrayed Moss in the same nuanced manner, revealing a man whose deeds brought him to ruin. These and numerous other parts have contributed to the development of Brolin as an actor whose work is motivated by metamorphosis and depth rather than the shallow allure of more traditional heroes.

Remaining Active in Television and Film
By pursuing television, another field that is becoming more and more recognized as essential to a long-term, prosperous career, Brolin has also been able to remain relevant. Brolin's star power extends beyond the big screen, as evidenced by his latest role in the television series Outer Range. The decision to switch to long-form television, which for more complex

character development, has turned out to be a calculated one and demonstrates Brolin's versatility as an actor.

Nowadays, a lot of well-known actors are thought to discover new opportunities for development on television, and Brolin has welcomed this change. He has been able to reach new audiences while keeping a high reputation because of his willingness to switch between film and television.

The Strength of Work Ethics and Authenticity

Brolin's perseverance is mostly due to his honesty and hard ethic. Brolin has remained loyal to himself, in contrast to many Hollywood actors who are sometimes preoccupied with upholding a particular image. He has frequently discussed the value of authenticity in both his personal and professional life. Many people may relate to him because of his willingness to be vulnerable, particularly when talking about personal issues like addiction. He also adds an authentic element to his work that appeals to viewers.

What longevity in Hollywood means has been redefined by Brolin's capacity to reinvent himself, his dedication to constant self-improvement, and his refusal to settle for past achievements. Success in Hollywood can be built over decades, sustained through hard work, and defined by an actor's ability to evolve. Josh Brolin has demonstrated this by staying relevant through reinvention, choosing a diverse range of roles, and staying true to his craft.

Inspiring the Next Generation

Josh Brolin's career is an inspiration to the upcoming generation of actors, directors, and creatives in addition to being a monument to his skill and tenacity. Brolin has demonstrated the value of perseverance, genuineness, and creativity throughout his career; these are traits that those who aspire to work in the entertainment sector can utilize as they forge their own routes to achievement. His narrative provides insightful guidance on overcoming setbacks, accepting new challenges, and being loyal to one's artistic vision.

Accepting Difficulties and Overcoming Misfortune
The fact that Brolin overcame hardship in both his personal and professional

lives is among the most potent facets of his legacy. Brolin's experience serves as a reminder to aspiring actors and creatives that failures are inevitable in the business world and that one's success is frequently determined by how one handles setbacks rather than how many they encounter.

Brolin had difficulties along the way. Brolin experienced a period of uncertainty and was frequently typecast or denied significant opportunities, despite his early performances in movies such as The Goonies and The Lost Boys: The Tribe. He struggled with addiction and the demands of celebrity, but instead of letting these obstacles stop him, he embraced them as inspiration to develop as a person and an actor. Brolin's story is a powerful illustration of how tenacity and a readiness to face one's inner demons can lead to success for anyone struggling in their professional or personal life.

Brolin's openness about his experiences with addiction also offers encouragement to anyone who might be going through similar difficulties. His candor regarding his recuperation and the benefits it has brought to his life serves as a potent reminder that no matter where one starts, change is achievable.

The Strength of Adaptability and Reinvention

Brolin's career serves as an example of flexibility, demonstrating that reinvention is not only a Hollywood survival tactic but also an essential component of sustaining long-term success. Brolin's versatility, willingness to try new things, and ability to play a wide range of parts provide young actors just starting in the business with a model for how to remain relevant in the ever-changing entertainment industry.

Brolin has demonstrated that an actor can stay at the forefront of the industry by consistently reinventing themselves, whether it is by switching from young, romantic roles to grizzled, morally complex characters in dramas like American Gangster and No Country for Old Men or by entering popular superhero movies like Deadpool 2 and Avengers: Infinity War.

Aspiring actors can benefit much from this lesson on flexibility. With new trends, genres, and technology appearing each, the entertainment sector is always evolving. Brolin's career demonstrates that the secret to a consistent and changing presence in the industry is to embrace change rather than fight it.

Pursuing Creative Freedom and Passion Projects

The value of pursuing passion projects and exercising creative freedom is another important lesson that Brolin teaches the next generation. Hollywood is frequently preoccupied with large budgets and financial success, but Brolin has always looked for parts and endeavors that push his creative boundaries. Brolin has demonstrated that genuine job fulfillment comes from artistic expression rather than merely pursuing fame or fortune, whether it is through collaboration on personal projects that push limits or working with visionary directors like the Coen brothers, Quentin Tarantino, or Ridley Scott.

This strategy serves as a reminder to aspiring actors and filmmakers that pursuing meaningful projects and maintaining creative integrity can be just as, if not more, significant than aiming for financial success. By putting his artistic goals ahead of his financial interests, Brolin has created a collection of work that reflects his love of telling stories, which viewers find incredibly compelling.

The Value of Cooperation and Guidance
Brolin has had the honor of collaborating with some of Hollywood's most renowned performers and directors throughout his career. He has demonstrated the importance of surrounding oneself with the best in the

industry through his work with directors such as Joel and Ethan Coen, Ridley Scott, and Quentin Tarantino, as well as his costarring roles with well-known actors like Tommy Lee Jones and Javier Bardem.

Brolin's career serves as a reminder to aspiring actors of the value of working with gifted people who can push and encourage them, as well as learning from mentors. He has also functioned as a kind of mentor, using his position in Hollywood to help and mentor up-and-coming artists while providing them with insightful advice on how to succeed in the business.

For the next generation, this focus on teamwork rather than rivalry is essential. Brolin's experience demonstrates that relationships, guidance, and a desire to collaborate toward shared creative objectives are more important for success than working alone.

Staying True to Oneself and Grounded
Brolin's ability to maintain his authenticity and groundedness in the face of the fame and pressure that come with being a Hollywood star is maybe one of the most admirable features of his career. Brolin has made it apparent during his ascent to prominence that his values—such as family, self-awareness, and personal development—are what really count. His approach to his work and personal life demonstrates that, even while Hollywood success is amazing, it's even more crucial to preserve one's identity and originality.

Brolin's example provides a different route for young individuals entering a field that frequently prioritizes celebrity over substance: one where self-awareness, humility, and authenticity are key components. His life serves as a reminder that being true to oneself and one's basic principles is just as important as receiving praise.

Making a Deep Impact on the Sector

The projects Brolin has sparked and the actors he has coached already demonstrate his impact on the next generation. He has demonstrated that an actor's influence is not solely determined by box office profits but also by the legacy they leave behind, both in terms of the work they produce and the lives they influence, by supporting up-and-coming creative voices and staying committed to his profession.

His career serves as evidence that being relevant in Hollywood requires not only temporary fame but also ongoing adaptation, development, and pursuit of new creative challenges. Brolin's career serves as a guide for people aspiring to be like him on how to leave a lasting legacy that goes beyond celebrity and benefits the profession and the wider world.

Conclusion

Josh Brolin's incredible career is proof of the strength of authenticity, resiliency, and reinvention in the face of Hollywood's constant change. From his breakthrough performance in The Goonies to his legendary depiction of Thanos in the MCU, Brolin has proven to be a remarkable actor who can adapt to a wide variety of roles in different genres while remaining loyal to his craft. Aspiring artists everywhere can learn from and be inspired by his path from an unknown young actor to one of the most reputable names in the business.

Brolin's tale is about the lessons he's learned and shared along the road, not just the awards and box office triumphs. He is a role model for anyone navigating the difficulties of their job because of his desire to take on new challenges, his unshakable work ethic, and his candor about overcoming personal struggles. Brolin has demonstrated that perseverance, genuineness, and a commitment to development are more important for long-term success in Hollywood than simply skill, whether it is through his partnerships with renowned filmmakers, his devotion to his trade, or his pursuit of passion projects.

Brolin's legacy will surely encourage the upcoming generation of actors, directors, and creatives to pursue their paths with bravery and tenacity as he continues to push boundaries in both cinema and television. His career serves as evidence that one may redefine what it means to make a lasting effect in a field that is continuously changing by having enthusiasm, flexibility, and tenacity. In addition to creating a remarkable body of work, Josh Brolin has changed the definition of longevity in Hollywood and will have a lasting impact on the business for years to come.

Printed in Great Britain
by Amazon